# EAT LIKE A LOCAL- DENVER

*Denver Colorado Food Guide*

Libby Thompson

**CZYK**
P U B L I S H I N G

CZYK Publishing Since 2011.

Eat Like a Local

Lock Haven, PA
All rights reserved.
ISBN: 9798662601994

# BOOK DESCRIPTION

Are you excited about planning your next trip? Do you want an edible experience? Would you like some culinary guidance from a local? If you answered yes to any of these questions, then this Eat Like a Local book is for you. Eat Like a Local - Denver by Author Libby Thompson offers the inside scoop on food in Denver, CO. Culinary tourism is an important aspect of any travel experience. Food has the ability to tell you a story of a destination, its landscapes, and culture on a single plate. Most food guides tell you how to eat like a tourist. Although there is nothing wrong with that, as part of the Eat Like a Local series, this book will give you a food guide from someone who has lived at your next culinary destination.

In these pages, you will discover advice on having a unique edible experience. This book will not tell you exact addresses or hours but instead will give you excitement and knowledge of food and drinks from a local that you may not find in other travel food guides.

Eat like a local. Slow down, stay in one place, and get to know the food, people, and culture. By the time you finish this book, you will be eager and prepared to travel to your next culinary destination.

# OUR STORY

Traveling has always been a passion of the creator of the Eat Like a Local book series. During Lisa's travels in Malta, instead of tasting what the city offered, she ate at a large fast-food chain. However, she realized that her traveling experience would have been more fulfilling if she had experienced the best of local cuisines. Most would agree that food is one of the most important aspects of a culture. Through her travels, Lisa learned how much locals had to share with tourists, especially about food. Lisa created the Eat Like a Local book series to help connect people with locals which she discovered is a topic that locals are very passionate about sharing. So please join me and: Eat, drink, and explore like a local.

# TABLE OF CONTENTS

16. On-the-Go Burritos
Meat-Free
17. Endless Options
18. Vegetarian
19. Meatless Wings
20. Vegan

Subs
21. Snarf's Sandwiches
22. Cheba Hut

Denver's Best Burgers & Hot Dogs
23. Cherry Cricket
24. Biker Jim's
25. Park Burger

Bars, Breweries & Tavern Fare
26. 10 Barrel Brewing
27. Rock Bottom
28. Blake Street Tavern
29. Historians

Pizza
30. Cosmo's
31. Giordano's
32. Blue Pan

BONUS TIP 1: Seafood (In A Landlocked State!)

Wine Bars
BONUS TIP 2: Postino
BONUS TIP 3: Barcelona Wine Bar

Late Night Fare
BONUS TIP 4: The Hornet
BONUS TIP 5: Ian's Pizza

Indoor Markets
BONUS TIP 6: Keep It Together!

Best Rooftops
BONUS TIP 7: Avanti
BONUS TIP 8: Irish Rover
BONUS TIP 9: Linger
BONUS TIP 10: The Source Hotel

Dessert
BONUS TIP 11: D Bar
BONUS TIP 12: Little Man Ice Cream
BONUS TIP 13: Sweet Action
BONUS TIP 14: Even More Ice Cream!
BONUS TIP 15: Get Social
BONUS TIP 16: Get Tea

# DEDICATION

This book is dedicated to my sister, Ally, who is always up to try something new, whether that requires a plane ticket or just a drive to a new diner. You will always be my adventure buddy!

# ABOUT THE AUTHOR

Libby is a middle school English teacher who lives in Denver, CO. She loves getting outside into Colorado's mountains to snowboard, snowshoe and hike. During her summers off she spends her time exploring outside of Colorado's borders, leading student trips and trying out local cuisine across the world.

Libby has lived in Colorado all her life, and in Denver for over four years. She has always found connection through food – connection.

# HOW TO USE THIS BOOK

The goal of this book is to help culinary travelers either dream or experience different edible experiences by providing opinions from a local. The author has made suggestions based on their own knowledge. Please do your own research before traveling to the area in case the suggested locations are unavailable.

**Travel Advisories**: As a first step in planning any trip abroad, check the Travel Advisories for your intended destination.
https://travel.state.gov/content/travel/en/traveladvisories/traveladvisories.html

# FROM THE PUBLISHER

Traveling can be one of the most important parts of a person's life. The anticipation and memories that you have are some of the best. As a publisher of the *Eat Like a Local*, Greater Than a Tourist, as well as the popular *50 Things to Know* book series, we strive to help you learn about new places, spark your imagination, and inspire you. Wherever you are and whatever you do I wish you safe, fun, and inspiring travel.

Lisa Rusczyk Ed. D.
CZYK Publishing

*"People who love to eat are
always the best people."*

– Julia Child

**M**any travelers make their way to Colorado
for the outdoor opportunities – there are
endless ways to play outside whether it's
summer or winter in Colorado, and Denver is a
reasonable drive from some excellent skiing, hiking
and more! Outdoor recreation is impossible without
proper fuel, and Denver's dining scene makes loading
up for your outdoor adventure an exciting experience
in itself.

There is truly something for everyone here, and
that may be why Denver has attracted such a vast
span of new locals in recent years. With more variety
in our residents we've also acquired more variety
when it comes to our food offerings, and locals
couldn't be more proud of that.

Even as a Denver local having lived here for years,
there are many restaurants still on my list to try and I
hope your adventurous spirit will lead you to food
that I haven't even gotten to enjoy yet! For the days
that require more planning, I hope my overview of

Denver's genres, go-tos and local favorites helps you find joy and diversity in Denver cuisine like I have.

Denver
Colorado, USA

# Denver Climate

|           | High | Low |
|-----------|------|-----|
| January   | 49   | 20  |
| February  | 49   | 21  |
| March     | 58   | 29  |
| April     | 65   | 35  |
| May       | 73   | 45  |
| June      | 86   | 55  |
| July      | 92   | 61  |
| August    | 90   | 59  |
| September | 82   | 50  |
| October   | 68   | 37  |
| November  | 57   | 27  |
| December  | 47   | 19  |

## GreaterThanaTourist.com

Temperatures are in Farenheit degrees.
Source: NOAA

# 1. GETTING AROUND

One perk of Denver's layout is that everything is relatively close together and when it isn't, there are plenty of local bus lines to connect the dots. A main connector between Capitol Hill and LoDo is 16th Street Mall, which is a beautiful pedestrian strip with a Free Mall Ride. Between the Mall Ride, buses, and of course the up-and-coming motorized scooters, there is often no need for Lyft or Uber.

# 2. DENVER WEATHER

Locals in Denver joke that if you don't like the weather here, all you need to do is wait five minutes. It's true that Colorado residents have enjoyed sunny mornings only to greet snow in the afternoon. We do get all four seasons here, but summers and winters are mild in comparison with Midwest or coastal U.S. cities. Denver doesn't get rain often, but in the summer there can be afternoon storms that sneak up on you!

With this in mind, wear or bring layers and plan for a few climate changes as you explore. Be sure to wear sunscreen, too – patio dining in the mile-high city means you're one mile closer to the sun, and we get 300 days a year of sunshine here in Colorado!

# 3. DENVER HISTORY

Denver began as a goldmining town and has history rooted in adventure, beer, and the railroad. The city offers a wide variety of historical attractions and walking tours for history junkies and those interested in the Gold Rush!

If you visited Denver ten years ago, some of the high-end eateries and steakhouses would still stand. As Denver has grown in popularity and diversity, more creative eateries and modern takes on food have made a name. Now, the food scene is full of variety and fun – without sacrificing the quality of those old-timey steakhouses.

# 4. LOCAL CULTURE

One of the many beautiful aspects of Denver is the variety of backgrounds the residents here represent. The vast majority of people living in Denver were raised in another state and likely have an interesting backstory to share. In general, Denverites are friendly and open to conversation. At restaurants as well as bars, don't forget to tip your server!

Denver is an up-and-coming city because of new job opportunities, local policy, and proximity to outdoor activities. It's rare to meet a local who doesn't enjoy a day floating on a reservoir, rafting, or embarking on a mountain adventure. In any group of friends you'll find a few climbers and at least one skier. Denver has an eclectic mix of neighborhood vibes that formed from so many people moving here from all over the country. Locals have created a relaxed but refined West-coast-meets-East-coast intersection, where upscale meets low-key.

# 5. HOW TO PAY

Nearly every restaurant in Denver accepts credit and debit

cards, and generally servers will take your card to the back to scan it as opposed to bringing a card reader to your table. If you're traveling with a group and will need the bill split, it's best to ask your server about it before you begin ordering so that they can more easily keep track of each tab, and save you both the headache of any back-and-forth with the bill at the end. Some smaller restaurants may not have the capability to split bills, so preparing for that answer off the bat is smart as well; keep track of what you order, put the meal on one person's card (yay, rewards points!) and use Venmo, Paypal or Cashapp to reimburse whomever paid.

I know of two places that do not accept cards and only take cash: Vine Street Pub and Voodoo Donuts. Both are absolutely worth a visit, but come prepared! Vine Street Pub does have an ATM, but fees will depend on your bank. Incredibly, Vine Street Pub will also take an "I Owe You" – a true show of trust in their community of customers.

# 6. DO YOUR HOMEWORK!

Ownership changes, hidden gems get so hidden they close down, and quality can ebb and flow. I hope this guide is a helpful starting point for your food-based adventures in Denver, but be sure to look into more current reviews of these restaurants or check out menus online to ensure it's up your alley and still operating in the same spot! Most Denver restaurants have websites or at least Facebook or Yelp pages where you can check on recent experiences and quality.

# 7. CALL AHEAD

Unless you're with a very large group, most of these restaurants are likely to have a wait time of less than an hour. If you're a larger group or are on a tight schedule, call ahead or check out OpenTable to see if you can make a reservation. In areas like LoDo and RiNo, checking in at the host stand and popping over to a bar next door is fairly easy, so even your wait won't feel like time lost. Most restaurants take your phone number and send an automated text when your table is ready, so you won't have to stand awkwardly in the foyer while you wait! Some restaurants are purely first-come first-served, but it's always worth a call to check.

# 8. MAIN AREAS DOWNTOWN

A few of the main downtown neighborhoods are LoDo (Lower Downtown), LoHi (Lower Highlands), RiNo (River North), Cap Hill, Uptown, and South Broadway. We'll keep our focus here, although there is plenty of delicious food to enjoy elsewhere, too! Most locals will define "downtown" as a combination of LoDo, Cap Hill, and RiNo, but many of the best places to eat are on South Broadway.

LoDo, also known as the Ballpark area, is a main point of attraction for young people looking to enjoy bars and nightlife. Coors field is located here, so on days with baseball games, the area is generally full to the brim with sports enthusiasts and fair-weather fans alike. If you arrived from the airport on the light rail, you likely arrived at Union Station, another main landmark of the neighborhood. Visit this area for great bar food, fun cocktails or a place to dance. If you're heading here, leave the car where you're staying – parking is expensive and difficult in this downtown area.

LoHi is directly across the highway from LoDo and features some of the best views and unique menus. It's easy to walk across the bridge there from LoDo, or grab an Uber. While there is some street parking in LoHi, it can be time-consuming and difficult to find. I generally opt to walk or Uber if I'm headed out there.

RiNo is a bit North of LoDo and is sometimes referred to as Five Points. Many of the establishments on this side of town are newer, but now there is no shortage of great food and drink to be found there! RiNo is best for breweries, food trucks and patio beers. On warm weekends, Denver locals flock to RiNo for brewery hopping and soaking up the sun on a patio.

Parking in RiNo is a usually easier than in LoDo, but busy nights can lead to lots of circulating blocks looking for a spot on the street. Motorized scooters are popular in this area of town and are a great option for hopping from place to place!

Cap Hill and Uptown aren't the most walkable areas of town, but they are home to a few gems I will discuss in following tips. The volume of restaurants in this area is low, but the quality is very high! If you prefer driving, these will be the easiest areas to park.

South Broadway is home to many long-standing bars and pubs as well as a few new and trendy spots like Canopy and Punch Bowl Social – both great sources of entertainment! Park a few blocks off of Broadway, on Lincoln or Sherman, for low-stress, free street parking. This is a great area for a more low-key night out – somewhere between dancing in LoDo and chill brewery hopping in RiNo!

# SEE IT ALL

## 9. VIEWS

For a view of downtown, you've got to go a bit outside it. LoHi is a great area for rooftop dining because it's right across the highway from the downtown area, giving a great view of the skyline. Two more neighborhoods with plenty of rooftop bars – some with mountain views - are RiNo and South Broadway. I'll be sure to call out locations featuring great rooftops as we go, but venturing out in any of those neighborhoods will leave you with plenty of options!

## 10. START THE DAY

Denverites love to brunch, especially when the weather's nice! On any given sunny weekend, patios are filled with locals enjoying mimosas, biscuits, grits and more!

# 11. BRUNCHING WITH A CREOLE TWIST

Two of the best brunch destinations in Denver happen to take on a Creole style of cuisine Lucille's and Sassafras. Both have multiple locations and ample seating space, so there's often no wait – but even when there is, it's worth it! At both spots, don't miss the beignets and the delicious jams.

The Lucille's menu is full of filling, hearty meals, most of which come complete with a large, flaky homemade biscuit. Their grits come in varieties like cheddar and jalapeno cheddar, and every variation of eggs benedict is a tasty option. If you're someone who enjoys a boozy brunch, Lucille's is a safe bet between their fruity cocktails and perfectly spiced Bloody Mary. There are even tropical rum or vodka-based juice drinks if you're really looking to kick off a party day!

At Sassafras, enjoy your preferred variation of biscuits and gravy (there's even a vegetarian option!) or go with another creole favorite like a po' boy or shrimp and grits! Sassafras's menu is also complete with plenty of lunch options, if breakfast dishes don't get you going. Sassafras's Colfax location is easy to miss, but don't pass it by! It's adorably decorated, large inside with two floors, and servers are exceptionally friendly. Do you ever wake up so hungry that the thought of waiting in line for brunch makes you want to cry? Those are the Sassafras days! Plenty of tables and quick service make for speedy delivery of delicious food.

# 12. THE PERFECT FLAKE

If creole isn't your style but biscuits are, head down South Broadway to visit Denver Biscuit Company. This southern-style establishment is open all day and serves biscuits in every form. Try a biscuit sandwich or a biscuit plate, or even a French toast or strawberry shortcake biscuit! Though most of the seating is inside the large brick establishment, there are a few street-facing spots to enjoy your meal in the sun.

# 13. ON A ROLL

Who doesn't love a good warm cinnamon roll? Butcher Block Café, located in the RiNo neighborhood, is a little hole-in-the-wall with plenty to love. Their jumbo, homemade cinnamon roll comes topped with a dollop of butter and is perfect for sharing with the table to top off a delicious breakfast omelette or burrito!

# 14. DONUTS!

Voodoo Donut is the best-known donut spot because of its tongue-in-cheek menu items and creative toppings, from bacon to fruity pebbles. They've even got a namesake donut: the Voodoo Doll is a doll-shaped donut with raspberry filling and chocolate frosting – stabbed by a pretzel stake. Shop their merchandise to take home a tee or mug featuring their creepy top-hatted mascot. Plan ahead to pick up here, because lines are often a few customers deep and can even wind right out the door. Be sure to bring cash as they do not accept cards.

If one good thing came from COVID-19, it's Pandemic Donuts! These visually pleasing, Instagrammable donuts are home cooked by a couple who lost their jobs due to the pandemic and managed to make the best of it. Visit their website to order and set up pickup.

Staying a bit south of Denver? The Donut in Centennial serves donuts as well as bear claws, cinnamon rolls and more! Stop by for a low-key morning complete with coffee and free Wi-Fi.

# 15. DENVER'S FAVORITE BREAKFAST BURRITO

Start your day at Onefold for a flavorful and filling breakfast burrito. These are jam-packed with egg, potato, your choice of meat, and more, and they glean added flavor from being prepared in duck fat. For a meat-free (and not duck fat-fried) option, simply order the vegetarian or vegan burrito. A local's advice: don't skip the smother! Any variation of their breakfast burrito is flavorful and moist as is, but smothering in pork or vegetarian green chili really takes it up a notch.

Seating inside Onefold is limited, so this is a great option for takeout. In addition to burritos, Onefold serves a unique variety of other breakfast and lunch dishes like Bacon Fried Rice, Breakfast Quesadillas, and Tacos Consome. Travel is all about trying new things, and Onefold is a great spot to expand your tasting repertoire. When you stop by, be sure to pick up a Vietnamese coffee or fresh squeezed orange juice!

# 16. ON-THE-GO BURRITOS

If you're busy exploring and don't have time to sit and enjoy something smothered, Santiago's and Bubba Chino's both serve up quick, spicy, filling breakfast burritos! Both are affordable (Bubba Chino's runs a two dollar burrito special until 11am every day!) and have various locations throughout the Denver area. Santiago's chili is some of the best around, and you can take it home by the jar!

# MEAT-FREE
# 17. ENDLESS OPTIONS

I am a Pescetarian, meaning the only meat I eat is fish (don't worry, I consulted plenty of my meat-eating friends to write this book!). In some places, a dietary restriction like that could be quite challenging and may mean a very limited list of restaurants would accommodate me. Not in Denver. Here, you'd be hard-pressed to find a restaurant that could not accommodate a vegetarian diet, and in most cases there are various vegan options as well. Perhaps this is due to a combination of the diversity of the city and the health-consciousness of Coloradoans in general.

Most menus include information on how to order items to be gluten-free, vegetarian or vegan. Our burger joints serve their own veggie patties or Impossible burgers, and I'll outline the best ones later the "Denver's Best Burgers & Hot Dogs" section. If you're traveling in a varied group with multiple different dietary needs, Denver is your ideal destination.

# 18. VEGETARIAN

When I moved to Denver after finishing college in Boulder, I knew hardly anyone in the city despite the proximity to my hometown and my college town. I lived alone in a tiny, old studio in Cap Hill and, like many early-20s recent grads, I was still discovering my place and establishing my community. Living only blocks from City O' City, I knew I had to try it out. It quickly became my go-to for meeting up with new friends, getting to know my coworkers, and showing my family what Denver's all about. City O' City, with its unapologetic personality, attention to detail, and comforting vegetarian dishes, was the first restaurant that made me feel truly at home in Denver.

Located in Cap Hill just blocks from the capital building, this trendy brick restaurant serves up delicious food for breakfast, lunch and dinner – and it's all completely meatless. Some dishes feature meat substitutes, like seitan wings or cauliflower "chicken" and waffles, while other items on the menu are so packed with flavor that diners barely notice that meat's amiss! Other dietary restrictions like vegan and gluten-free are very well accommodated here, too. Vegetarians, I highly encourage you to drag your meat-eating friends and family here (I have many times!) to prove once and for all that a vegetarian diet does not mean eating salad for every meal!

For a genuine feel for Denver's personality, City O' City is a necessary stop. Its plant-heavy yet dark décor, the servers, and even the menu itself tell a story and leave diners wanting more. Even if you consider yourself a meat-eater, a stop by City O' City will give you a glimpse of Denver's heart.

# 19. MEATLESS WINGS

There are few things that challenge my pescetarianism more than chicken wings. Luckily, Denver is full of options to fulfill that craving. City O' City, mentioned above, is a top contender. Their wings are made of seitan, which is made from wheat gluten and mimics the tougher texture of meat better than cauliflower or other substitutes can. Barbecue sauce at City O' City is pretty sweet, and I always opt for half barbecue and half buffalo wings to keep some variety of flavors.

I'll highlight Fire on the Mountain more in depth later, but vegetarians absolutely need to know about this go-to wing spot serving multiple vegetarian options! One option is seitan, which come in orders of a few different sizes and come with sauces of your choosing (they make several and they are all amazing!). Seitan wings at Fire on the Mountain are cooked in the sauce, while their other meatless option, cauliflower wings, come plain with sauce on the side to dip in. Cauliflower wings here are very heavily battered and fried to perfection, but if you're sensitive to fried foods you may want to opt for the seitan.

For perfectly-fried, light and saucy cauliflower wings, head to Whiskey Tango Foxtrot in LoDo. This bar and restaurant isn't known for its vegetarian fare and serves a large and varied menu, but they've got the cauliflower wing game won! Watercourse's buffalo cauliflower is definitely worth a try as well.

# 20. VEGAN

If you're vegan and want to skip the stress of wondering what's in your meal, try out Watercourse in the Uptown area. Their menu is entirely plant-based, and their cauliflower wings are some of the best in town. Cashew mac and "cheese" is another fan favorite! Sit outside and people watch in Uptown as you enjoy a meal entirely free of animal products. If you've got a short wait, explore their small shop for sustainable products like bamboo straws, reusable straw cleaners, and Watercourse swag. Peak hours can be busy, but their late-night happy hour is a great way to end a day!

For a light breakfast or lunch, The Corner Beet in Cap Hill is a refreshing vegetarian and vegan café known for their toast and their acai bowls but also offering burrito bowls and salads for a healthy way to get your day started.

Looking for a plant-based pastry? Beet Box in Uptown is a vegan bakery offering sandwiches, pastries, bread, donuts and more. They even have gluten-free options!

## SUBS

## 21. SNARF'S SANDWICHES

Snarf's branding is almost as silly as its name, with adorable (or scary?) googly-eyed characters gracing their signage and sandwich bags. The Snarf's menu isn't huge, but their subs are delicious and filling! Whether you're looking for a good meatball parmesean or a vegetarian sandwich, Snarf's has you covered.

## 22. CHEBA HUT

In recent years Colorado has become recognizable as one of the few states with legal recreational marijuana, but even before then, Cheba Hut's menu was full of witty, weed-referencing titles. Even their sandwich sizes (nug, pinner, and blunt) play into their theme. Jokes aside, Cheba Hut's large menu features toasted subs in dozens of varieties – plenty of which are vegetarian!

## DENVER'S BEST BURGERS & HOT DOGS

## 23. CHERRY CRICKET

Located in LoDo just steps from Coors Field, Cherry Cricket is a lively burger joint with delicious appetizers and shakes (boozy and regular!) to boot. Start your meal with salty and tangy Cherry Bombs, or creamy Mac and Chesse bites. The menu features a variety of entrees, but locals know to go for the burger.

Even vegetarian and vegan diners can look forward to a burger here – they serve an Impossible burger, and they cook it to perfection! Try it topped with smoked cheddar and pineapple, or choose your favorite toppings from their exhaustive list.

# 24. BIKER JIM'S

This hot dog joint takes variety to a whole new level! Offerings include standards like all-beef and bacon cheddar brats, but also expand to wild boar, elk jalapeno cheddar, and rattlesnake and pheasant! They even serve a vegan dog. If you're looking for a new twist on the all-American meal, you've found it!

Biker Jim's is situated right downtown, where RiNo and LoDo intersect. Whether you're brewery-hopping in RiNo or about to catch a baseball game at Coor's Field, this is a great place to stop for a bite – and try something just a bit outside your comfort zone!

# 25. PARK BURGER

If you'd like a burger joint without all the frills and extras, Park Burger is a great bet. With four central locations, it's convenient no matter your day's itinerary and route. Burgers come on locally baked buns and are handcrafted fresh – including a house made veggie patty!

# BARS, BREWERIES & TAVERN FARE

# 26. 10 BARREL BREWING

10 Barrel Brewing is a triple threat: mouthwatering brews, delicious food, and a rooftop dining area! Head to the RiNo neighborhood to enjoy their craft beers, either inside in their expansive dining area, upstairs bar-style, or on their barrel-themed rooftop. Not until you make it to the roof and look back into the restaurant will you be able to see that the entryway is shaped just like a giant beer barrel!

There's something for everyone on their food menu, from thin-crust pizza to juicy hamburgers and fresh salads. Don't miss their Cucumber Sour, a refreshing local favorite! If you're looking for a place to fill time between meals, the atmosphere and appetizers at 10 Barrel make it a great spot to sit and chat without pressure to order a full meal. Many of their house beers are light and sour – try a flight and compare notes!

# 27. ROCK BOTTOM

If you're out for a shopping day on 16th Street Mall, this brewery on the mall is a perfect stop! Serving over a dozen small brew beers on tap, Rock Bottom's atmosphere is fun yet elevated. Large groups are well-served here because of the size of the dining room and the expansive menu. There is something for everyone at Rock Bottom, from tuna poke nachos to burgers to meatless entrees. Rock Bottom is one of my go-tos if I'm trying to cater to a group of picky or particular eaters and drinkers. Leave the car behind for an outing here, because parking near 16th Street can quickly become expensive and exhausting. If you need to drive, find a lot near Denver Pavilions instead of circling for street parking with time limits that will only impede your adventuring.

# 28. BLAKE STREET TAVERN

Located in LoDo near plenty of bars and the ballpark, Blake Street Tavern is a sports bar with plenty of personality. Come for the fun ambiance, stay for the beer and appetizers: nachos, wings, jumbo pretzels and quesadillas are all done right. Venture down to the basement area for arcade games and plenty of space to hang out, no matter the size of your group!

# 29. HISTORIANS

Yet another rooftop hangout, Historians is located on South Broadway near plenty of other eateries and bars to pop by. This is a great lunch option! Soak up the sun while you enjoy a sandwich or salad – and don't forget the beer! If you're visiting in colder months, the downstairs indoor seating area boasts a comfy, old-timey vibe. In warm weather, the rooftop patio is well worth the trip up the stairs. Views from Historians are breathtaking and include both the Rocky Mountains and the city of Denver itself.

# PIZZA

## 30. COSMO'S

Coloradoans all know and love Cosmo's pizza! Deliciously thin crust and perfect sauce-to-cheese ratio give this pizza joint its local favorite status. Cosmo's has two claims to fame: the spicy ranch (definitely worth the extra 50 cents per side) and the giant 24" pie. This beast of a pizza will easily feed a large group or provide leftovers for lunch tomorrow! The location isn't anything frilly or fancy, but Cosmo's is a great bet for pick-up or picnicking.

## 31. GIORDANO'S

For every person who craves thin-crust, New York-style pizza, there's another who'd prefer deep dish with plenty of cheese and sauce. If that's you, or if you're looking for a more comprehensive Italian menu, take a walk down 16th Street Mall to Giordano's! Order the Chicago Classic for an authentic slice, or build your own pizza. Be sure to schedule in a little extra time, since deep-dish takes longer to cook.

# 32. BLUE PAN

Delicious, cheesy crust and creative signature pies make Blue
Pan's Detroit style pizza a crowd favorite. Detroit style pizza has a thick crust and plenty of cheese. For those who do believe pineapple goes on pizza, the Sweety Pie (with pineapple, bacon, jalapeno and ricotta) will be the highlight of your day. The Koto Telluride is an exciting vegetarian option featuring creamy artichoke and spinach sauce!

As is the case with many Denver restaurants, Blue Pan leaves room for a variety of tastes and also offers thin New York style pizzas and a few options for Chicago-style. There's even a healthy selection of gluten-free pizzas on their menu!

# 33. WALNUT PIZZERIA

A well-known thin-crust pizza joint with a diverse set of beers on tap, this pizzeria is top-notch. Sit outside if you can, and enjoy the crackling fire pit in the evening. Though the façade is small, Walnut Pizzeria is also a hidden, small concert venue. Into the indie music scene? Maybe you'll catch a show while you're in town!

# 34. PIE HOLE

As the name suggests, Pie Hole is a no-frills, nothing-fancy,

greasy pizzeria that is guaranteed to hit the spot after a long day exploring the city. For lovers of thin-crust, this hole in the wall is a can't miss stop on South Broadway. Keep this location in your back pocket if you're planning a night out on South Broadway – they're open late, and there's nothing like a great slice of pizza at the end of a busy night!

If you opt for lunch or dinner here, head a few doors down afterward to top off the meal at Sweet Action ice cream!

## TACOS

# 35. TORCHY'S TACOS

Driving down South Broadway, you can't miss the huge, lit-up Torchy's Tacos sign. Consider its conspicuousness a favor – you truly do not want to miss these tacos or the excellent queso! Drinks here don't disappoint, either. Try a frozen house margarita for the perfect tangy touch for your taco feast.

Into breakfast tacos? Swing by Torchy's to start your day with a Migas or Ranch Hand taco for a morning done right. Not a meat eater? Try the satisfying Fried Avocado taco. The menu also includes a burrito and a salad, in case someone in your group isn't down for tacos. Order to your heart's desire because there's really only no way to go wrong at Torchy's – except by missing out on the chips and queso!

# 36. MACHETE

The LoDo area is packed with bars and breweries – don't forget to eat! Located right across from Union Station, Machete is known for strong tequila drinks and delicious tacos. Their menu is authentic and they've got tacos for anyone's taste. If you're into spicy food, be sure to try their flavor-packed sauces!

# 37. DOS SANTOS

Ask a local where to grab tacos, and most will suggest Dos Santos. Plan this one a bit in advance, because there is often a bit of a wait due to the intimate seating area. Grab margaritas by the pitcher and enjoy friendly service whether you're out on the patio or in the dining room.

Dos Santos is located in a quieter area of Uptown where you can get away from the bustle and take a stroll down the street while you wait for your table without bumping into many people. The restaurant itself may draw a crowd, but the area of town is a peaceful break from a busy day.

# 38. TACOS TEQUILA WHISKEY

With three convenient locations, there is no reason to miss out on the upbeat vibe and unbeatable tacos at Tacos Tequila Whiskey! Take advantage of their happy hour, from 3-6 nightly and all night on

Mondays! Featured cocktails like Palomas and margaritas are always flowing, and every variety of their street tacos is well-made. With a lively atmosphere perfect for getting the party started, Tacos Tequila Whiskey draws a varied crowd of young people enjoying drinks, and taco connoisseurs enjoying an artful meal.

# DIM SUM

# 39. WHAT TO EXPECT

Eating at a Dim Sum restaurant if you haven't before is worth a bit of an overview in preparation, since the dining experience looks different than many other restaurant styles. These restaurants may serve regular entrees, but show up during the hours they're serving Dim Sum for the fully authentic experience. Dim Sum is best with a larger group because it's served community style – everyone at the table can share in the meal, so having more people allows for everyone to try a larger variety of foods. When I go with just a couple friends, we always end up full before we're able to try all of the different varieties of dumplings we'd like to.

This is one of very few styles of food I don't recommend for vegetarians or vegans. As a pescetarian, I'm able to eat plenty at Dim Sum because there are tons of shrimp-based options in addition to the more-popular pork and beef varieties. If you eat at least fish, you'll leave satisfied, but completely meatless Dim Sum is more rare – there are a few desserts without meat, plus broccoli and seasoned cucumbers (which are delicious!). Another solution if there is a vegetarian in your group might be for them to order their own entrée off of the menu while the rest of the group goes for the Dim Sum-style meal.

Dim Sum is served early in the day (not a dinner outing) and mainly features dumplings and other bite-sized portions, served in small steamer baskets. Most dishes will include pork, shrimp, scallops, or beef. Instead of looking at a menu and ordering, diners get to choose what they'd like to try from push-carts circulating the restaurant. These come around on a constant basis, so you can choose a few plates, eat up, and determine how much more to try. The set-up can be a bit intimidating at first, but the kind servers are there to help you out as they circulate the carts and serve you the baskets. Enjoy the experience and try something new. Don't forget to order tea!

# 40. WHERE TO GO

Denver's best Dim Sum is in the Westwood area, about a ten-minute drive from downtown. There are two restaurants with very similar selection and quality: Super Star and Star Kitchen. Call ahead to see who is accepting reservations for the Dim Sum service. Wait times can be upwards of an hour on the weekends, but they're worth a wait. At either place, the fried shrimp balls, cucumbers, and cheese wontons never disappoint!

## WORLDWIDE

# 41. PHO

Pho is a Vietnamese soup that usually contains beef broth, rice noodles, and meat. It's generally served with a plate of add-ins like bean sprouts, basil, cilantro, jalapenos and lime. Load it up with all the toppings you'd like, then add sauces like hoisin and Sriracha to achieve your ideal flavor balance.

Much like Dim Sum, the best place to find quality pho is in the southwest area of Denver. Pho 555 and Pho 95 are local favorites and offer something for everyone, including vegetarian pho and delicious Boba tea! At Pho 555, enjoy a laid-back atmosphere and great service in a midsized dining room with a fish tank centerpiece.

# 42. ETHIOPIAN

There are quite a few options for Ethiopian food in Denver, making it convenient to try out this satisfying cuisine no matter where you're staying! Ethiopian food, like Dim Sum, requires some flexibility from guests who are used to eating in more Americanized restaurants. In most Ethiopian restaurants, guests do not use silverware but instead eat using the bubbly, pancake-like bread one which dishes are served. Communal-style eating is key here as well – and be ready for some spice!

Your choice of restaurant may depend mostly on convenience of location for you: check out Arada Ethiopian in Lincoln Park, The Ethiopian Restaurant in City Park, Mesob Ethiopian in Montclair, or Queen of Sheba in Park Hill! Whichever you choose, you're sure to have a unique experience and a warm and filling meal.

# 43. INDIAN

Little India is family-owned and offers large portions of Indian classics, from veggie korma to chicken Tikka Masala. The service in their dining room is friendly and quick, and the naan is a great addition to any meal. I'm a regular at the 6th Avenue location, and the servers there truly treat guests like family. They are thoughtful enough to remember usual orders and have even remembered to ask about my sister when I come in without her. Their consideration is absolutely reflected in the quality of the food as well. Looking for a lunch spot? Their lunch buffet offers delicious food, plenty of options, and unlimited portions.

Find delicious Himalayan food with authentic ambiance and an inspiring backstory when you head west to Golden for Sherpa House Restaurant and Cultural Center. The restaurant is family-owned and aims to serve authentic food while also educating guests about Sherpa culture, right down to the organization of the space and artifacts. For large groups, this is a great fit because there is ample seating space both indoors and outside, and the restaurant accepts reservations so you can be sure your wait time will be short.

# 44. SUSHI

Denver locals fall into one of two camps: Sushi Den or Go Fish. Both offer high-quality sushi at a fair price (though Sushi Den is slightly more expensive), and great service. The first main difference between the two is location. Sushi Den is located in south Denver, near the University, and is a short drive away from the action of downtown. Go Fish is more centrally located on South Broadway, near bars, shops, and other attractions. Each has their own ambiance: while Sushi Den offers a more elevated and classic experience, Go Fish is attached to a lounge that gets more at Denver's nightlife scene.

Choose your sushi spot based on what you're looking for today: a classy, purist sushi experience with fresh fish flown in daily? Go for Sushi Den. If you'd like a more relaxed atmosphere with a large menu and some specialty chilled sake, Go Fish is for you!

# 45. CONVEYOR BELT SUSHI

If both Sushi Den and Go Fish seem too pricy or fancy, Sushi-Rama is a more economical (and, arguably, more fun!) choice for sushi night! Sit at a booth or along the bar and watch as plates of sushi make their way toward you on the conveyor belt – then grab what you want! Menus are at each table to help add context to the labeled plates, and each plate is color-coded based on its price. At the end, your server will count your colored plates and charge you accordingly.

# 46. THAI

"Hole in the wall" might sound cliché, but the phrase is fully embodied here. Don't expect any frills here, however you'd be hard-pressed to find excellent Thai food for a price like this! Though the outside of the restaurant isn't much, Thai Monkey Club on South Broadway is the best Thai food in Denver by far. This is another great option if you're looking for takeout, but their dining room is clean and simple as well. A few favorites from the menu are pineapple curry and drunken noodles – but beware of the spice! With most dishes, waiters will ask for your spice preference on a scale of 1 to 6. If you are not used to eating very spicy Thai food, a 2 is the safest bet (I eat spicy food regularly…I like to order a 3 and always end up crying!). Cool down with a Boba tea and their delicious crab cheese wontons.

# 47. COLOMBIAN

La Chiva is a bit of a drive down South Broadway but is worth

the time, especially if you're looking for authentic Colombian fare. There are only a few Colombian restaurants in Denver, and La Chiva is by far the best. If you're a fan of Colombian food, you'll find all your favorites perfectly executed. Complete your meal with a Colombian drink, like a fresh-squeezed fruit juice or Pony Malta! If you've never tried Colombian, it's the ideal spot to get your first taste! Try their arepas or empanadas if you're not sure where to start. Classics like arroz con pollo are especially popular here.

If Denver's typical brunch scene isn't for you, try the brunch options at La Chiva! Too far of a drive? Find their food truck schedule and visit them on the go instead.

# 48. RAMEN

Mention of the word "Ramen" in Denver will always be met with the same refrain: Uncle. You'd be lucky to find Uncle without a line at the door. Even takeout can sometimes take upwards of an hour – but it's worth the wait. A second Uncle location opened recently, which should improve timeliness. No matter the wait, this is the best Ramen in Denver. Delicious broth, delicate noodles and all the heartiness you'd expect from a bowl of comfort food – Uncle has it all. Locals know that this is also the best place to grab Bao buns; their pork Bao buns are unmatched.

# 49. CREPES

As someone who studied in France, I am especially picky about my crepes and, let's be honest, it's tough to find a perfectly thin and ideally filled crepe here in the U.S. The best I've managed to find is at the Boulder Farmer's Market on Saturdays, and I often make the drive just for the breakfast crepe. Head to the Savory Saigon tent and order to your heart's content – I highly recommend their breakfast crepe, with basil cream sauce instead of hollandaise.

That one is savory, but there are plenty of options for sweet crepes, such as yogurt and berries or Nutella!

If a drive to Boulder is not on the itinerary, Crepes N' Crepes is located conveniently on 16th Street Mall and serves up a wide variety of yummy crepes, too! This is a great stop for lunch, breakfast, or a quick snack.

# 50. SOUTHERN DELIGHTS

Although many Denver residents generally concern ourselves with healthy eating, we're still human! No one can resist some barbecue or soul food every now and then. Welton Street Café in RiNo is both centrally located and affordable, without sacrificing quality. From wings and burgers to fried shrimp and fried chicken, they cover every soil food base. On 16th street mall, Boney's BBQ is your best chance for perfectly smoked meats and finger-licking sauces.

"Vegetarian" and "soul food" don't go together, right? Think again, then check out SoulNia, a pop-up and catering company where there's an emphasis on "colorful eating." If that doesn't work out, try a sides sampler at Boney's BBQ – who doesn't love filling up on macaroni and cheese?

# BONUS TIP 1: SEAFOOD (IN A LANDLOCKED STATE!)

Block off your Monday night, because Mondays are all-day happy hour at Jax Fish House! We may be landlocked, but at Jax the fish is fresh and well-prepared. Buy snow crab by the pound, oysters on the half shell and peel n' eat shrimp for the table. Pair with wine or beer from their extensive selection and eat to your heart's content!

Jax is a great choice for celebrating a special occasion – even with happy hour, it often ends up quite pricey, but it's worth every cent! Fresh seafood is not easy to come by in Colorado.

Inside of Denver Central Market you'll find more affordable seafood options like clam chowder and po' boys. If you're willing to go a bit outside of the city limits, Bonefish Grill also offers exceptional seafood flown in fresh daily.

WINE BARS

## BONUS TIP 2: POSTINO

Come for the wine, stay for the delicious bruschetta board! Now
with two locations, Postino is a trendy choice with chic decorations and delicious snacks. Their bruschetta board is the talk of the town – it will be gone quickly in a group of any size! The board comes with your choice of four types of bruschetta, and the menu features options like Salami & Pesto and Sweet & Spicy Pepper Jam with Goat Cheese. If you're with a large group, order a couple boards and try them all! Other fare to accompany your wine includes cheese boards, tuna tartare or crispy cauliflower. At the LoHi location, there is ample patio seating.

## BONUS TIP 3: BARCELONA WINE BAR

For a fun but classy evening outing – perhaps after dinner or before a bigger night out – spend some time at Barcelona wine bar! You'll have the most fun experience if you sit up at the bar itself, where neighbors and bartenders are likely to strike up a conversation. During peak hours, servers even walk on top of the bar to serve sangria directly into your mouth from a high-up pitcher! It may sound intimidating, but the delivery is so smooth you hardly have to try, and the drink is delicious – trust me, you want the free taste. Try out tapas like patatas bravas, potato tortilla or candied beets for to kick-start your appetite.

# LATE NIGHT FARE

# BONUS TIP 4: THE HORNET

Choosing a category for The Hornet posed quite a challenge, because they serve food all day long and their menu hosts such a variety of dishes that it fits under multiple buckets! The Hornet is a local favorite as far as brunch goes, serving up Mulemosas, Kombucha Mimosas, and Bloodies on a Budget to accompany their simple but scrumptious food menu.

As delicious as their food is during the day, nothing hits the spot like a late-night meal, and The Hornet is wisely open until 1am on Fridays and Saturdays. End your night out on South Broadway there with a snack like nachos or onion rings, or go all out for a burger, sandwich or even lobster mac and cheese. If you're up for a drink, the specialty cocktails at The Hornet are reason enough to visit – I recommend trying Been Stung One Too Many Times (and not just because it's funny to say).

## BONUS TIP 5: IAN'S PIZZA

If a night out dancing in LoDo made it onto your itinerary, you're required to end the night with a few slices of pizza at Ian's Pizza (hey, I don't make the rules!). Located right across the street from Coors Field and serving pizza by the slice, Ian's is a go-to for a quick bite and a lifesaver after a long night. Bars in Denver close at 2am and Ian's closes even later, making it a great last stop before turning in for the night.

# INDOOR MARKETS

# BONUS TIP 6: KEEP IT TOGETHER!

Denver Central Market, Broadway Market, Milk Market, and Zepplin Station all follow a similar layout and are great places to start an evening out. There is truly something for everyone, because each location features numerous rotating vendors as well as a full bar.

Each of these eateries is full of trendy indoor space and features plenty of outdoor seating, too. Start your day at Denver Central Market if you're loading up before hopping between RiNo's breweries, and use Milk Market the same way in LoDo. Zepplin Station is a great choice if you're heading to a concert at Mission Ballroom on RiNo's outskirts. Check out websites beforehand to see what vendors and restaurants are currently serving each market. At Zepplin Station and Milk Market, there are cute local shops on top of plenty of food options!

# BEST ROOFTOPS

## BONUS TIP 7: AVANTI

For an evening bite overlooking the city lights, head to Avanti in LoHi. This collective eatery features an ever-changing selection of restaurants, each with a unique menu. One longstanding favorite there is Quiero Arepas – don't miss out on their plantain-packed arepas!

Avanti's balcony and outdoor area is perfect for enjoying a cocktail or full meal while admiring the Denver skyline. There are food booths both upstairs and downstairs, with one central bar. Take your time to browse menus before committing – there are so many delicious options to choose from!

## BONUS TIP 8: IRISH ROVER

On South Broadway, a great rooftop option is the Irish Rover. Whether it's warm or cold during your visit, the rooftop is a great bet! There are misting machines in the summer to help keep guests cool, while heaters and plastic screens keep diners warm and shielded from the wind in cooler months. A lively and bustling atmosphere is always there to greet you at Irish Rover! It's open late and it's always worth a stop if you're bar hopping in the area. If you're traveling with a dog, their backyard patio is a dog-friendly spot to enjoy a beer and a meal.

# BONUS TIP 9: LINGER

Maybe Colorado isn't well-known for ghosts, but if we have any, they're definitely inside of Linger. Previously O'Linger's Mortuary, Linger is situated in LoHi. Outdoors, there are beautiful views. Indoors, there's food served where corpses were once prepared (or so it's rumored here in Denver).

Even without the view of the city, the ample space, and the interesting lore, Linger's menu alone makes it worth the visit. Denverites frequent their rooftop for brunch, but there's a delicious lunch and dinner menu as well. Set up like a world tour with sections for Americas & Europe, Africa & Middle East, and Asia, this menu features dishes you won't find anywhere else in Colorado. Ever tried watermelon gazpacho or Moroccan Chicken B'stilla? Now's your chance! Whatever you do, do not skip the Bao buns!

# BONUS TIP 10: THE SOURCE HOTEL

This is an upscale, boutique hotel hosting a variety of food options. From pizza downstairs to an artisanal bakery and a barbecue joint, the Source is loaded with options from top to bottom. Down at the bottom of the hotel, they serve beers from a small New Belgium Brewing side project, where guests get to try some of New Belgium's best sour beers.

The Woods Restaurant and Bar is a local's favorite due to its rooftop view as well as its food. For a mountain view instead of a look at the skyline, the Source is your best bet. Enjoy a cocktail or beer while overlooking the Rocky Mountains – a great location for a romantic outing!

## DESSERT

# BONUS TIP 11: D BAR

Though known and named for its desserts, D Bar serves delicious food at every course and also features a to-go bakery. This is one restaurant where reservations are definitely a good idea, and booking early is safest. Looking for a date spot? You've found Denver's favorite! If you can't get a reservation, make a point to go by their bakery for a delicate macaron or a light and airy slice of Funfetti cake.

It should go without saying, but if you're eating dinner at D Bar, be sure to leave room for dessert! Some options from the dessert menu are familiar (but still exquisitely done), like the crème brulee, churros, or milk and cookies. Other items are much more creative, like "Why So Cereal," a plate featuring Cinnamon Crunch Souffle, Fruity Pebble donuts and more! Come ready for surprises, as their dessert menu rotates seasonally and is always creatively crafted.

# BONUS TIP 12: LITTLE MAN ICE CREAM

If you haven't waited in a very long line at Little Man Ice Cream, you haven't really experienced Denver! Walk down from Linger, Postino or any other LoHi locale to top off your night at Little Man. You can't miss it – it's marked by a 28 foot tall steel cream can flaunting its name. The shop is open until midnight and offers all outdoor seating and the freshest flavors around.

# BONUS TIP 13: SWEET ACTION

A contender for the best ice cream in Denver, this ice cream shop features unconventional flavors that carry the imagination and the palate to new places. The smell of their home-baked waffle cones wafts through the air, and the hipster vibe of the South Broadway neighborhood is impossible to ignore. All of the ice cream flavors are seasonal and rotating, so you'll never have the same experience twice.

# BONUS TIP 14: EVEN MORE ICE CREAM!

There is certainly no shortage of ice cream shops in Denver, and I've never found one to disappoint! In City Park West, check out Smith + Canon for something spicy like El Chupacabra (a spicy chocolate flavor), Dew Sabi (honeydew meets wasabi) or Strawbanero (strawberry habanero). Stay a while to enjoy the patio or take a look around the shop for a souvenir.

MyKings Ice Cream is a newly opened ice cream shop in the Skylan area that's packed with joy through and through. This shop keeps things fresh and exciting by serving up 12 rotating flavors. Their claim to fame? Cereal milkshakes! Get a taste of childhood with a Cinnamon Toast Crunch or Fruity Pebbles milkshake.

# BONUS TIP 15: GET SOCIAL

Punch Bowl Social on South Broadway is paradise for any "child at heart." The first thing you'll see when you enter Punch Bowl Social is their dining room, where guests can enjoy tasty appetizers or a whole hearty meal. Most locals don't come for the food, though – we're there for the games!

Downstairs there's a large bar area with classic cocktails (they make a great Moscow Mule!), which connects to a full bowling alley! Step up your darts game in one of their backlit, digitally scored booths, or head upstairs for ping-pong or foosball. Every local Denver couple has a photo on the iconic "I love you so much" wall – find it on your way upstairs!

# BONUS TIP 16: GET TEA

Are we in London, or in Denver's Brown Palace? Afternoon tea at the Brown Palace is a can't-miss activity for anyone looking for the royal treatment. Complete with finger sandwiches and tea imported straight from England, tea at the Palace is a treat for visitors of all ages! If tea isn't your thing, don't rule out the Brown Palace yet. Their dining room is a step above the rest and is a high-end option for any special occasion or reunion.

TeaLees Tea Co. is an excellent, more laid-back alternative to the Brown Palace. Enjoy afternoon tea and a relaxed chat in the teahouse and bookstore located in RiNo. They describe their atmosphere as Afro-centric and offer chocolates and specialty drinks (some alcoholic) in addition to their expansive selection of tea trays. To book a special occasion or high tea, visit their website and call in advance.

# BONUS TIP 17: GET FANCY

Longing for a taste of the past at an upscale restaurant? The Capital Grille in LoDo offers an elevated air and steaks cooked to perfection. Make a reservation online of by phone and enjoy a decadent night on the town!

# BONUS TIP 18: GET FIRE-Y

For the lovers of dipping sauces and the lovers of appetizers, Fire on the Mountain is an excellent choice for take-out or dine-in. Wings are their specialty, but vegetarians needn't fret: there are not one but two variations of vegetarian wings: cauliflower and seitan! Even non-vegetarians can feel good about eating here because their chicken is sourced responsibly, as recognized by the Good Food 100 List.

Did I mention their wing sauce variety? Sauces, sauces, sauces! If you're indecisive like me, their sauce tasting station by the checkout counter will be a life saver. My recommendation? Try the raspberry habanero sauce for a great mixture of spice and tang. Look for their specials – sometimes you can catch a 75-cent wing deal!

# BONUS TIP 19: GET SUNSHINE

Located on one of RiNo's most bustling streets, Improper City is the perfect spot for soaking up some sun, getting a few hours of work in, or just chatting! Coffee flows all morning and any Italian Roast connoisseur will be impressed. Food trucks line the patio area and are ever-changing, always a surprise! Despite the huge space, Improper City always feels packed with groups of friends in the evenings or work-from-homers during the day. Play a game of corn hole or enjoy a creative cocktail before exploring the rest of RiNo's breweries and patios.

Can't get enough food trucks? Head down the street from Improper City to Finn's Manor, which hosts four food trucks and two bar locations. This one is a fair-weather destination because there isn't much indoor space. When it's nice outside, locals and visitors spend hours eating, drinking, and dancing to live music at Finn's!

# BONUS TIP 20: KEEP AN OPEN MIND

Denver is full of adventurous eaters and creative chefs. Don't write things off without first trying them or getting a second opinion! The best way to get a true taste of Denver is to stay away from bigger chain restaurants that might feel familiar – and that can be hard when you're away from home. Don't leave Colorado without tasting something new – but no local will judge you for turning up your nose to Rocky Mountain Oysters (don't ask!).

# BONUS TIP 21: KEEP COMING BACK

Our city is changing and growing rapidly – this is the fact to which we owe our diversity and much of the tangible excitement that comes from being here. Change leaves space for innovation and risk-taking and has resulted in our wide variety of genres and experiments around town. While I hope this guide is helpful to anyone dining in Denver, I hope you also expand your horizons and look for what's new in town – there is bound to be something even more creative and even more tasty each time you come back to visit us.

# OTHER RESOURCES:

https://www.tripadvisor.com/Restaurants-g33388-Denver_Colorado.html

https://www.denver.org/denver-meetings-conventions/decide-on-denver/denver-dining-scene/must-try-restaurants/

https://denver.eater.com/

https://303magazine.com/2020/06/black-owned-businesses-denver/?fbclid=IwAR2NstQAOagEi1BpAL3elf7_F5bylJF9HH0dqC92x4uJ3IlyNxwxdI5seDg

# READ OTHER BOOKS BY CZYK PUBLISHING

*Greater Than a Tourist- St. Croix US Birgin Islands USA: 50 Travel Tips from a Local* by Tracy Birdsall

*Greater Than a Tourist- Toulouse France: 50 Travel Tips from a Local* by Alix Barnaud

Children's Book: *Charlie the Cavalier Travels the World* by Lisa Rusczyk

# Eat Like a Local

Follow *Eat Like a Local on* Amazon.
Join our mailing list for new books
http://bit.ly/EatLikeaLocalbooks

Printed in Great Britain
by Amazon